by Iain Gray

LangSyne
PUBLISHING
WRITING *to* REMEMBER

LangSyne
PUBLISHING
WRITING *to* REMEMBER

Vineyard Business Centre,
Pathhead, Midlothian EH37 5XP
Tel: 01875 321 203 Fax: 01875 321 233
E-mail: info@lang-syne.co.uk
www.langsyneshop.co.uk

Design by Dorothy Meikle
Printed by Ricoh Print Scotland

ISBN 978-1-85217-408-8

Mullan

MOTTO:
To live is to conquer.

CREST:
A sword supported by a crescent.

NAME variations include:
Mac Maoláin *(Gaelic)*
Ó Maoláin *(Gaelic)*
Ó Meallain *(Gaelic)*
MacMullan
MacMullen
Mullen
Mullens
Mullin
Mullins
O'Mullan
O'Mullen
O'Mullin

Chapter one:

Origins of Irish surnames

According to an old saying, there are two types of Irish – those who actually are Irish and those who wish they were.

This sentiment is only one example of the allure that the high romance and drama of the proud nation's history holds for thousands of people scattered across the world today.

It's a sad fact, however, that the vast majority of Irish surnames are found far beyond Irish shores, rather than on the Emerald Isle itself.

The population stood at around eight million souls in 1841, but today it stands at fewer than six million.

This is mainly a tragic consequence of the potato famine, also known as the Great Hunger, which devastated Ireland between 1845 and 1849.

The Irish peasantry had become almost wholly reliant for basic sustenance on the potato, first introduced from the Americas in the seventeenth century.

When the crop was hit by a blight, at least 800,000 people starved to death while an estimated two million others were forced to seek a new life far from their native shores – particularly in America, Canada, and Australia.

The effects of the potato blight continued until about 1851, by which time a firm pattern of emigration had become established.

Ireland's loss, however, was to the gain of the countries in which the immigrants settled, contributing enormously, as their descendants do today, to the well being of the nations in which their forefathers settled.

But those who were forced through dire circumstance to establish a new life in foreign parts never forgot their roots, or the proud heritage and traditions of the land that gave them birth.

Nor do their descendants.

It is a heritage that is inextricably bound up in the colourful variety of Irish names themselves – and the origin and history of these names forms an integral part of the vibrant drama that is the nation's history, one of both glorious fortune and tragic misfortune.

This history is well documented, and one of the most important and fascinating of the earliest sources are *The Annals of the Four Masters*, compiled between 1632 and 1636 by four friars at the Franciscan Monastery in County Donegal.

Compiled from earlier sources, and purporting to go back to the Biblical Deluge, much of the material takes in the mythological origins and history of Ireland and the Irish.

This includes tales of successive waves of invaders and settlers such as the Fomorians, the Partholonians, the Nemedians, the Fir Bolgs, the Tuatha De Danann, and the Laigain.

Of particular interest are the *Milesian Genealogies*,

because the majority of Irish clans today claim a descent from either Heremon, Ir, or Heber – three of the sons of Milesius, a king of what is now modern day Spain.

These sons invaded Ireland in the second millennium B.C, apparently in fulfilment of a mysterious prophecy received by their father.

This Milesian lineage is said to have ruled Ireland for nearly 3,000 years, until the island came under the sway of England's King Henry II in 1171 following what is known as the Cambro-Norman invasion.

This is an important date not only in Irish history in general, but for the effect the invasion subsequently had for Irish surnames.

'Cambro' comes from the Welsh, and 'Cambro-Norman' describes those Welsh knights of Norman origin who invaded Ireland.

But they were invaders who stayed, inter-marrying with the native Irish population and founding their own proud dynasties that bore Cambro-Norman names such as Archer, Barbour, Brannagh, Fitzgerald, Fitzgibbon, Fleming, Joyce, Plunkett, and Walsh – to name only a few.

These 'Cambro-Norman' surnames that still flourish throughout the world today form one of the three main categories in which Irish names can be placed – those of Gaelic-Irish, Cambro-Norman, and Anglo-Irish.

Previous to the Cambro-Norman invasion of the twelfth century, and throughout the earlier invasions and settlement of those wild bands of sea rovers known as the Vikings in the eighth and ninth centuries, the population of the island was relatively small, and it was normal for a person to be identified through the use of only a forename.

But as population gradually increased and there were many more people with the same forename, surnames were adopted to distinguish one person, or one community, from another.

Individuals identified themselves with their own particular tribe, or 'tuath', and this tribe – that also became known as a clann, or clan – took its name from some distinguished ancestor who had founded the clan.

The Gaelic-Irish form of the name Kelly, for example, is Ó Ceallaigh, or O'Kelly, indicating descent from an original 'Ceallaigh', with the 'O' denoting 'grandson of.' The name was later anglicised to Kelly.

The prefix 'Mac' or 'Mc', meanwhile, as with the clans of the Scottish Highlands, denotes 'son of.'

Although the Irish clans had much in common with their Scottish counterparts, one important difference lies in what are known as 'septs', or branches, of the clan.

Septs of Scottish clans were groups who often bore an entirely different name from the clan name but were under the clan's protection.

In Ireland, septs were groups that shared the same name and who could be found scattered throughout the four provinces of Ulster, Leinster, Munster, and Connacht.

The 'golden age' of the Gaelic-Irish clans, infused as their veins were with the blood of Celts, pre-dates the Viking invasions of the eighth and ninth centuries and the Norman invasion of the twelfth century, and the sacred heart of the country was the Hill of Tara, near the River Boyne, in County Meath.

Known in Gaelic as 'Teamhar na Rí', or Hill of Kings, it was the royal seat of the 'Ard Rí Éireann', or High King of Ireland, to whom the petty kings, or chieftains, from the island's provinces were ultimately subordinate.

It was on the Hill of Tara, beside a stone pillar known as the Irish 'Lia Fáil', or Stone of Destiny, that the High Kings were inaugurated and, according to legend, this stone would emit a piercing screech that could be heard all over Ireland when touched by the hand of the rightful king.

The Hill of Tara is today one of the island's main tourist attractions.

Opposition to English rule over Ireland, established in the wake of the Cambro-Norman invasion, broke out frequently and the harsh solution adopted by the powerful forces of the Crown was to forcibly evict the native Irish from their lands.

These lands were then granted to Protestant colonists, or 'planters', from Britain.

Many of these colonists, ironically, came from Scotland and were the descendants of the original 'Scotti', or 'Scots', who gave their name to Scotland after migrating there in the fifth century A.D., from the north of Ireland.

Colonisation entailed harsh penal laws being imposed on the majority of the native Irish population, stripping them practically of all of their rights.

The Crown's main bastion in Ireland was Dublin and its environs, known as the Pale, and it was the dispossessed peasantry who lived outside this Pale, desperately striving to eke out a meagre living.

It was this that gave rise to the modern-day expression of someone or something being 'beyond the pale'.

Attempts were made to stamp out all aspects of the ancient Gaelic-Irish culture, to the extent that even to bear a Gaelic-Irish name was to invite discrimination.

This is why many Gaelic-Irish names were anglicised with, for example, and noted above, Ó Ceallaigh, or O'Kelly, being anglicised to Kelly.

Succeeding centuries have seen strong revivals of Gaelic-Irish consciousness, however, and this has led to many families reverting back to the original form of their name, while the language itself is frequently found on the fluent tongues of an estimated 90,000 to 145,000 of the island's population.

Ireland's turbulent history of religious and political strife is one that lasted well into the twentieth century, a landmark century that saw the partition of the island into the twenty-six counties of the independent Republic of

Ireland, or Eire, and the six counties of Northern Ireland, or Ulster.

Dublin, originally founded by Vikings, is now a vibrant and truly cosmopolitan city while the proud city of Belfast is one of the jewels in the crown of Ulster.

It was Saint Patrick who first brought the light of Christianity to Ireland in the fifth century A.D.

Interpretations of this Christian message have varied over the centuries, often leading to bitter sectarian conflict – but the many intricately sculpted Celtic Crosses found all over the island are symbolic of a unity that crosses the sectarian divide.

It is an image that fuses the 'old gods' of the Celts with Christianity.

All the signs from the early years of this new millennium indicate that sectarian strife may soon become a thing of the past – with the Irish and their many kinsfolk across the world, be they Protestant or Catholic, finding common purpose in the rich tapestry of their shared heritage.

Chapter two:

The Shining Ones

With roots buried deep in the ancient soil of the Emerald Isle, the genealogy of the Mullans is as complex as it is rich and colourful.

Carefully untangling the genealogical strands, however, it is possible to discern that, in its original Gaelic forms such as Ó Maoláin and Ó Meallain, it was present from earliest times throughout all four of the island's ancient provinces of Ulster, Munster, Leinster and Connacht – with the latter becoming their main territory.

Not all of the various tribal groupings who later adopted the Mullan name – derived from the Gaelic 'maol', meaning 'bald' or 'tonsured' – were necessarily related, but what their descendants of today have in common is a pedigree shot through with vibrant Celtic myth and legend.

Legend holds that the first bearer of the name was a descendant of one of the earliest kings of Connacht.

One branch of the Ó Maoláins, or Mullans as they became known, were part of a tribal grouping known as the Gaileanga and the Luighne, who held territory in present day Co. Meath.

The Gaileanga and Luighne also included what became the clans of Cullen, Dolan, Kavanagh, Lynam, Mannion, Quinn and others, and, curiously, what they all have in common is that their Coats of Arms feature what is known as the Crescent of Danu, and a sword.

According to legend the first tribe to inhabit Ireland were the Fomorians although, rather improbably, they are said to have dwelled mainly in the sea.

Invasion then came in the form of the Partholonians who, after a bitter and bloody struggle for supremacy over the Fomorians that lasted close on 300 years, were wiped out in an epidemic.

Then came the tribe of the Nemed, followed by the Fir Bolgs who, after inter-marrying with the Fomorians, held sway over the island until the arrival at an undetermined date of the Tuatha De Danann, who eventually overthrew them after a succession of fierce battles.

Later becoming established in Connacht, and known as the People of Danu, and the Shining Ones, it is from them that the Mullans and other clans are believed to descend.

It was from the Irish moon goddess known as Danu, or Dana, that the Tuatha De Danann took their name.

Legend relates how Eoghan Mor, a king of the Tuatha De Danann gods, lost his arm in battle and how his silversmith magically crafted him a new one.

The sword featured in the Coats of Arms of the Mullans and other members of the Gaileanga and the Luighne feature the sword of Eoghan Mor, while the crescent, symbolic of the moon, is also representative of the goddess Danu.

As noted above, the derivation of the Mullan name is

from a word meaning 'bald' or 'tonsured' – with tonsured indicating a holy man, such as a priest of the Druidic cult, and, later, a priest of the Church.

This is quite apt, in view of the fact that there was a noted monastic branch of the Mullans.

This branch was associated with a number of religious communities throughout Ireland that included Ros Comnain, Clonfert, Clonmacnoise and Ceanannus, better known as Kells. He also carried out missionary work in Scotland.

There was also a significant presence of Mullans in the province of Ulster, particularly in present day Co. Donegal, where they were one of the main septs of Clann Conchuir Magh Ithe – indicating a descent from Niall Noíghiallach, better known to posterity as the great fourth century warrior king Niall of the Nine Hostages.

These Ulster Mullans functioned for centuries as a warrior class, subordinate to the overall power of the O'Cahans (O'Kanes), while their name survives on the Donegal landscape to this day in the form of the township of Mullan.

Rather confusingly, bearers of the Mullan name of wholly different origins are also to be found in Ulster today.

This came about through the policy known as 'plantation', the settling of loyal subjects of the Crown on the lands held by intransigent native Irish started during the reign from 1491 to 1547 of Henry VIII, whose Reformation effectively outlawed the established Roman Catholic faith throughout his dominions.

This settlement of loyal Protestants in Ireland continued throughout the subsequent reigns of Elizabeth I, James I (James VI of Scotland) and Charles I.

Among these settlers were MacMillans/Macmillins from Scotland, who later adopted the forms of 'MacMullan' or Mullan.

This explains why the Mullans of today are recognised as a sept, or sub-branch, of the proud Scottish Clan MacMillan.

From earliest times, ancestors of the Mullans of today were at the forefront of resistance to invasion of their native shores, not least invasion in the form of the Vikings.

Mainly of Norwegian origin, it was in the closing years of the eighth century A.D. that their sinister longboats, their sails often adorned with the motif of a black raven, first appeared off Irish shores, and the monastery of St. Patrick's Island, near Skerries in present day Co. Dublin was looted and burned to the ground.

Raids continued along the coastline until they made their first forays inland in 836 A.D., while a year later a fleet of 60 Viking vessels sailed into the River Boyne.

An indication of the terror they brought can be found in one contemporary account of their depredations and desecrations.

It lamented how 'the pagans desecrated the sanctuaries

of God, and poured out the blood of saints upon the altar, laid waste the house of our hope, trampled on the bodies of saints in the temple of God, like dung in the street.'

By 841 A.D. the Vikings, or Ostmen as they were also known, had established a number of strongholds on the island, but their raids began to ease off before returning with a terrifying and bloody vengeance in about 914 A.D.

They met with a determined resistance from the native Irish, most notably in the form of the forces of the powerful confederation of clans known as the Southern Uí Neill, of which the Mullans were part.

The Irish suffered a resounding defeat at the battle of Dublin in 919 A.D. and it was not until just over thirty years later that the raids gradually came to an end.

It was during this period that the Mullan ancestor, Maelan, described in the ancient annals as Lord of the Gaileanga, was slain in a particularly vicious encounter with the Vikings.

In much later centuries, bearers of the Mullan name also fought for the doomed cause of the exiled Stuart monarch James II (James VII of Scotland), following the Glorious Revolution of 1688 that brought the Protestant William of Orange and his wife Mary to the throne, while they were also active in the equally futile rebellion against the power of the English Crown in 1798.

Chapter three:

The wearing of the green

One particularly infamous bearer of the Mullan name, and one whose daring exploits are still spoken of today throughout the Ulster counties of Derry and Tyrone, was the outlaw Shane "Crossagh" O'Mullan.

Born at some point in the latter decades of the seventeenth century near Ballynascreen, his nickname of "Crossagh" indicated 'pock-marked' – although by all accounts he did not suffer from any facial blemish, and in fact was renowned for his handsome appearance.

The nickname, it is thought, one also shared by his father and brothers, may have derived from a distant ancestor who was distinctly pockmarked.

He was a young man when, evicted from the family farm for non- payment of rent, he took to the hills and roads of Derry and Tyrone to pursue the life of an outlaw, a life known as "the wearing of the green".

Relentlessly pursued by the authorities, he became renowned as an Ulster version of England's Robin Hood – robbing the rich to give to the poor.

His name survives on the landscape today in the form of the wild and beautiful Glenshane Pass, while Shane's Leap recalls an incident when, closely pursued, he jumped from a waterfall on Burntollet River and, despite breaking a leg in the process, still managed to make good his escape.

Near the village of Feeny, roughly five miles southwest of Dungiven, is what is still known to this day as the General's Bridge – so named in recognition of another of his famed exploits when he and his band ambushed a force of Government troops, including the general who commanded them.

They robbed them of their valuables, including their horses, and, forcing them to strip to their underwear, they had to ignominiously walk all the way back to Derry.

But the forces of the law eventually caught up with the bold Shane when, in 1722, he and two of his sons were betrayed by an informer.

The three were hanged at the Diamond, in Derry, and Shane later buried at Banagher Old Church.

According to a persistent legend, a foal skin bag, filled with gold coins that Shane had amassed during his outlaw career, still lies buried somewhere in the local landscape.

His exploits are also remembered through a popular folk song, one verse of which reads:

Shane Crossagh was a ploughboy
That ploughed in Ballynascreen
And now he is an outlaw for the wearing of the green.
'Twas in the Sperrin mountains far, far from
Ballynascreen
They set the bloodhounds on his track
For the wearing of the green.

In later centuries, bearers of the Mullan name and its spelling variants have gained honours and distinction on several fields of conflict.

One of nineteen American service personnel to have received the Medal of Honor, the nation's highest military honour, on two separate occasions, Patrick Mullen was born in 1897 in Baltimore, Maryland.

Enlisted in the U.S. Navy during the Civil War of 1861 to 1865, the boatswain's mate was awarded his first Medal of Honor after a boat expedition up Mattox Creek, Virginia, in March of 1865, when, under heavy fire and after assisting a wounded officer, he managed to disperse the enemy lining the bank by accurate fire from a howitzer.

His second Medal of Honor was awarded only two months later when, serving as a boatswain's mate aboard the *U.S.S. Don*, he managed to pick up the crew of a picket boat that had become swamped; he died in 1897.

Yet another Medal of Honor recipient was Hugh P. Mullin, born in 1878 in Richmond, Illinois, and who died in 1948.

It was while serving as a seaman aboard the *U.S.S. Texas* during the Philippine-American War, that, in November of 1899 at Hampton Roads, Virginia, while the vessel was taking on coal, at great risk to himself he rescued a fellow seaman who had fallen overboard.

Born in 1869 in Grahamstown, South Africa, Charles Mullins was a recipient of the Victoria Cross (V.C.), the highest award for bravery in the face of enemy action for British and Commonwealth forces.

A captain in the Imperial Light Horse (Natal) during the Second Boer War of 1899 to 1902, it was at the battle of Elandslaagte in October of 1899 that he and another officer, who was also awarded the V.C. for his actions on the day, rallied their men to carry out a successful flanking attack on the enemy.

Later promoted to the rank of major, he died in 1916.

Born in 1892 in Portland, Oregon, but moving with his family at the age of two to Moosomin, Saskatchewan, George Mullin was an American-Canadian recipient of the V.C.

A sergeant in the Princess Patricia's Canadian Light Infantry, Canadian Expeditionary Force, during the First World War, it was in October of 1917 at Passchendale, Belgium, that he single-handedly charged and captured an enemy pillbox that had been inflicting heavy casualties on his comrades.

Appointed Sergeant at Arms of the Saskatchewan Legislature in 1934, he served as a captain in the Veteran's Guard during the Second World War.

He died in 1963, and his V.C. is now on display at the Museum of the Regiments in Calgary, Alberta.

One particularly intrepid bearer of the Mullan name was the American civil engineer, explorer and soldier John Mullan, who was born in 1830 in Norfolk, Virginia.

Graduating from West Point military academy in 1852, he was a member of an expedition that explored what was then the newly created Washington territory.

Promoted to First Lieutenant in the U.S. Army in 1855, his skill as a topographical engineer led to him being tasked with the construction of a wagon road, across the Rockies, between Fort Benton, Montana, and Fort Walla Walla, Washington.

The route is known to this day as the Mullan Road.

Later serving as Catholic Commissioner for Indian Missions, which defended the rights of Native Americans, he died in 1909; in addition to the Mullan Road, other places named in his honour include the township of Mullan, Idaho.

One example of the many bearers of the Mullan name who left their native Ireland and found fame in the nation in which they settled, was John Mullan, who was born in Dublin in 1871 and who died in 1941.

Immigrating to Australia at the age of 18, he worked in a succession of jobs that included railway worker, clerk and miner.

A labour activist, he became an organiser of the Charters Towers Miners' Union and Australian Workers' Union.

Elected to the Queensland Legislative Assembly as the Labor member for Charters Towers in 1908, and to the Australian Senate five years later as a Labor Senator for

Queensland, he served from 1920 to 1929, and again from 1932 until 1940, as Attorney General.

Also in the often cut-throat world of politics, Charles Heron Mullan, better known as C.H. Mullan, was the influential Northern Irish Unionist politician and judge who was born in 1912 and died in 1996.

Serving with the Royal Navy during the Second World War and being elected a member of the British Parliament in 1946 for Co. Down, he was a member of the Ulster Unionist Council until he was appointed a judge in 1960.

Chris Mullin, born in 1947 in Chelmsford, Essex, is the British Labour Party politician, journalist and author who served as the Member for Parliament for Sunderland South from 1987 to 2010.

His 1982 political novel, *A Very British Coup*, was adapted for television six years later, while other political posts he held include chairman of the Home Affairs Select Committee, from 1997 to 1999, and Parliamentary Under Secretary at the Department for International Development.

Chapter four:

On the world stage

Bearers of the Mullan name, in all its rich variety of spellings, have achieved fame through a number of pursuits and endeavours.

Born in 1959 in Peterhead, in the northeast of Scotland, but later moving with his family as a child to the Mosspark area of Glasgow, **Peter Mullan** is an award-winning actor, screenwriter and filmmaker.

Beginning his acting career after studying economic history and drama at Glasgow University, he was closely involved for a time with Scotland's left-wing theatre movement, in particular the *7:84* and the *Wildcat Theatre* companies.

His earliest film appearances include the 1994 *Shallow Grave*, the 1996 *Trainspotting* and, from 1995, Mel Gibson's *Braveheart*, while as a screenwriter and director he has produced a number of films that include the 1998 *Orphans*, which won an award at the Venice Film Festival, as did his 2002 *The Magdalene Sisters*.

He also produced and wrote the screenplay for the gritty 2011 *Neds*, based on the gang culture of Glasgow in the 1970s.

Other acting roles include the 1998 *My Name is Joe*, for which he won the Best Actor Award at the Cannes Film

Festival, and the 2010 *Harry Potter and the Deathly Hallows*.

Making her screen debut at the age of nine in the 1998 *Hideous Kinky*, **Carina Mullan** is the English actress whose other film roles include the 2001 *The Musketeer* and who has also appeared in the British television medical drama *Casualty*.

Bearers of the Mullan name have also excelled, and continue to excel, in the highly competitive world of sport.

In Gaelic football, **Ciarán Mullan** is the talented player who was born in 1984 in Drumsurn, Co. Londonderry.

Playing club football for St Matthew's Drumsurn, he also plays for Co. Derry and was a member of the Derry team that won the 2008 National League, beating Kerry.

Also in Gaelic football, and another player from Derry, **John Mullan** was born in 1923 in Galvin, near Dungiven.

One of Derry's top players of the 1940s and 1950s, he helped the team to take the prestigious Dr McKenna Cups in both 1947 and 1954; regarded as one of Derry's best ever players, the forward, who played club football for most of his career with St Canice's Dungiven, died in 2008.

From Gaelic football to the boxing ring, **Harry Mullan**, born in 1946, was the Irish journalist and boxing writer who edited *Boxing News* from 1977 to 1996 and who was inducted into the International Boxing Hall of Fame six years after his death in 1999.

In the sport of rugby, **Mike Mullins**, born in Auckland in 1970 of joint Irish and Maori parentage, is the former New Zealand rugby union footballer who, because of his Irish ancestry through his father, qualified to play for the Republic of Ireland – earning six caps between 1999 and 2003.

Also in the rough and tumble of rugby union, **Matt Mullan**, born in 1987 in Brighton, is the English loosehead prop and occasional hooker who has played for the Worcester Warriors since 2005 and who has been a member of the England national team since 2010.

In the popular Gaelic sport of hurling, **John Mullane**, born in 1981 in Waterford, is the Irish player who began playing for the Waterford senior inter-county team in 2001.

Described as a legend in the world of horse racing following his death in 2010 at the age of 91, **Paddy Mullins** was the Irish racehorse trainer who, in a career that lasted more than 50 years, had a number of notable successes that included four Irish National winners and six Cheltenham Festival wins.

These included the Cheltenham Champion Hurdle in 1984 and the Cheltenham Gold Cup in 1986, with Irish jockey Jonjo O'Neill riding Dawn Run.

His legacy is continued through his sons Tom, Tony and Willie Mullins.

Trainer of the 2005 British Grand National Winner, Hedgehunter, Willie, who was born in 1956, is also a former six times Irish amateur champion jockey.

Across the ocean from Ireland to the United States, **Christopher Mullin** is the retired basketball player who has the distinction of being one of only two players in basketball history to win the prestigious Haggerty Award – given to the best college player in the New York City area – on three occasions, 1983, 1984 and 1985.

Born in 1963 in Brooklyn and a player for teams that include the Golden State Warriors and the Indiana Pacers, he was also a member of the U.S. men's basketball team that won the gold medal at the 1984 and 1992 Olympic Games.

On the fields of European football, **Jimmy Mullen**, born in 1923 in Newcastle-upon-Tyne and who died in 1987, was the England international striker who played from 1937 to 1960 with Wolverhampton Wanderers.

In soccer, as European football is known in North America, **Brian Mullan**, born in 1978 in Mineola, New York, is the midfielder who has played for teams that include Colorado Rapids, Los Angeles Galaxy and Houston Dynamo and who, to date, has been capped six times for the U.S. national team.

From sport to the written word, **Don Mullan**, born in 1956 in Derry, is the Northern Irish author whose 1997 book *Eyewitness Bloody Sunday – The Truth*, formed the basis of the 2002 film *Bloody Sunday*.

The book and film concern the highly controversial events of January 1972 when twenty-six civil rights protestors and bystanders were shot dead by British troops in the Bogside area of Derry during a march organised by the Northern Ireland Civil Rights Association.

Mullan, who from 1994 until 1996 was involved with the Concern Worldwide humanitarian agency, was invited as a special guest to the inauguration of Nelson Mandela as President of South Africa in recognition of his activism on behalf of the anti-apartheid movement.

In poetry, **Harryette Mullen**, born in 1953 in Florence, Alabama, is the American poet and literary scholar whose 2002 collection *Sleeping with the Dictionary*, was nominated for America's National Book Award, the Book Critics Circle Award and the *Los Angeles Times* Book Prize.

Winner of the 2010 Jackson Poetry prize for Poets and Writers, her other best-selling works include her 1981 *Tree Tall Woman* and her 2002 *Blues Baby*.

In the equally creative world of art, **George Mullins** was the noted Irish painter who, before embarking on his career as a landscape painter, was employed in painting the trays and lids for snuff boxes; he died in 1775, aged 35.

From art to music, **Larry Mullen, Jr.** is the drummer and one of the founding members of the internationally successful Irish rock band U.2.

Born in Dublin in 1961, he founded the nucleus of the band, along with school friends Paul "Bono" Hewson and David "The Edge" Evans after posting a notice on his school bulletin board stating: "drummer seeks musicians to form band."

The band, to date, has won 22 Grammy Awards, while Mullen added the suffix of Jr., indicating 'junior' to his name after his father, also named Larry, kept receiving tax demands meant for his son.

Born in 1964 in Cincinnati, Ohio, Nicole Coleman-Mullen, better known as **Nicole C. Mullen**, is the award-winning gospel singer and songwriter who, to date, is the only African American to win the Dove Award for Song of the Year.

This was for her 2001 *Redeemer*, while other Dove Awards include the 2005 award for Female Vocalist of the Year.

From gospel music to jazz, William Mullins, better known as **Bitsy Mullins**, was the American trumpeter born in 1926 in Pine Bluff, Arkansas, who played for luminaries including the Tommy Dorsey Band, Buddy Rich, Tony Bennett, Sammy Davis, Jr., Lena Horne and Dean Martin.

Inducted into the Arkansas Jazz Hall of Fame in 1995, he died in 2003.

Also in jazz, **Jim Mullen**, who was born in 1945 in Glasgow, is the jazz-rock guitarist who has played with bands that include The Average White Band and Brian Auger's Oblivion Express.

Along with tenor saxophonist Dick Morrissey, he co-founded the band Morrissey-Mullen, and is the recipient of a number of awards that include those for Best Guitarist in the British Telecom Jazz Awards in 1994, 1996 and 2000.

One particularly remarkable bearer of the Mullan name was the Northern Irish evangelist **Willie Mullan**, who was born in 1911 in Newtonards, Co. Down.

His autobiography, *Tramp After God*, relates how he had spent a number of years as a down-and-out and tramp, suffering from alcoholism and involved in crime before, in 1953, he took up the Christian message and began preaching in Lurgan Parish Church.

His sermons proved so popular that they were audiotaped and distributed throughout the world to the extent that, more than 30 years after his death in 1980, they still enjoy a massive Christian appeal.

Key dates in Ireland's history from the first settlers to the formation of the Irish Republic:

circa 7000 B.C.	Arrival and settlement of Stone Age people.
circa 3000 B.C.	Arrival of settlers of New Stone Age period.
circa 600 B.C.	First arrival of the Celts.
200 A.D.	Establishment of Hill of Tara, Co. Meath, as seat of the High Kings.
circa 432 A.D.	Christian mission of St. Patrick.
800-920 A.D.	Invasion and subsequent settlement of Vikings.
1002 A.D.	Brian Boru recognised as High King.
1014	Brian Boru killed at battle of Clontarf.
1169-1170	Cambro Norman invasion of the island.
1171	Henry II claims Ireland for the English Crown.
1366	Statutes of Kilkenny ban marriage between native Irish and English.
1529-1536	England's Henry VIII embarks on religious Reformation.
1536	Earl of Kildare rebels against the Crown.
1541	Henry VIII declared King of Ireland.
1558	Accession to English throne of Elizabeth I.
1565	Battle of Affane.
1569-1573	First Desmond Rebellion.
1579-1583	Second Desmond Rebellion.
1594-1603	Nine Years War.
1606	Plantation' of Scottish and English settlers.

1607	Flight of the Earls.
1632-1636	Annals of the Four Masters compiled.
1641	Rebellion over policy of plantation and other grievances.
1649	Beginning of Cromwellian conquest.
1688	Flight into exile in France of Catholic Stuart monarch James II as Protestant Prince William of Orange invited to take throne of England along with his wife, Mary.
1689	William and Mary enthroned as joint monarchs; siege of Derry.
1690	Jacobite forces of James defeated by William at battle of the Boyne (July) and Dublin taken.
1691	Athlone taken by William; Jacobite defeats follow at Aughrim, Galway, and Limerick; conflict ends with Treaty of Limerick (October) and Irish officers allowed to leave for France.
1695	Penal laws introduced to restrict rights of Catholics; banishment of Catholic clergy.
1704	Laws introduced constricting rights of Catholics in landholding and public office.
1728	Franchise removed from Catholics.
1791	Foundation of United Irishmen republican movement.
1796	French invasion force lands in Bantry Bay.
1798	Defeat of Rising in Wexford and death of United Irishmen leaders Wolfe Tone and Lord Edward Fitzgerald.

1800	Act of Union between England and Ireland.
1803	Dublin Rising under Robert Emmet.
1829	Catholics allowed to sit in Parliament.
1845-1849	The Great Hunger: thousands starve to death as potato crop fails and thousands more emigrate.
1856	Phoenix Society founded.
1858	Irish Republican Brotherhood established.
1873	Foundation of Home Rule League.
1893	Foundation of Gaelic League.
1904	Foundation of Irish Reform Association.
1913	Dublin strikes and lockout.
1916	Easter Rising in Dublin and proclamation of an Irish Republic.
1917	Irish Parliament formcd after Sinn Fein election victory.
1919-1921	War between Irish Republican Army and British Army.
1922	Irish Free State founded, while six northern counties remain part of United Kingdom as Northern Ireland, or Ulster; civil war up until 1923 between rival republican groups.
1949	Foundation of Irish Republic after all remaining constitutional links with Britain are severed.